1. The Art Gallery, a gift to Bristol by Mr W.H. Wills. The tram is travelling towards Park Row, with Park Street behind the horse and cart. The horse trough and fountain are an interesting feature on the side of the road on this card by Harvey Barton, posted in August 1912.

2. Looking in the opposite direction towards Queens Road. The arch-way next to the Art Gallery is the entrance to the H.Q. of the Rifle Volunteers, later the 4th Gloucester's. Published by Harvey Barton in the same series, and sent in April 1912.

CLIFTON

3. The Royal Promenade, or better known as Queens Road, the elegant frontage to the shops still recognisable today, and still a busy shopping area. Postcard postally used in May 1915.

4. From the Victoria Rooms in the opposite direction along Queens Road. Shops include Maynards, Duck Son & Pinker, and B. Maggs & Co. in this view from the late 1930s. The Tram Posts are in the centre of the road, with a tram entering Queens Road in the distance.

5. Queens Road looking towards the city in 1924. The corner of Richmond Terrace on the right near Lennards shop, with the clock in the tower which was destroyed in the 1939-45 war during an air raid.

6. Queens Road. The Victoria Rooms and a bustling street scene. A tram, bicyles and a No.20 bus near the corner with Queens Avenue. This view also in the mid 1920s.

7. Victoria Rooms. The foundation stone was layed in 1838, and the building completed in 1841, this view with the railings still around it, with the newly erected statue to commemorate the Boer War in front. The statue was unveiled in March 1905, and the postcard sent in September 1905.

8. Whiteladies Road, at the junction with St. Pauls Road and to the right Tyndalls Park Road, the houses with verandah's now owned by the B.B.C. This postcard was posted in April 1905.

CLIFTON

9. Whiteladies Road near the corner with Oakfield Road, tram No.8, en route for Durdham Downs from the tramway centre. Note the ladies in long skirted fashions, near the postbox, in this view dated about 1906.

10. Whiteladies Picture House on the corner of Melrose Place. Double bill of films showing: Constance Talmadge in "Learning to Love" and Virginia Valli in "Why The Woman". Luncheons, dainty tea's and dinners available in the cinema restaurant.

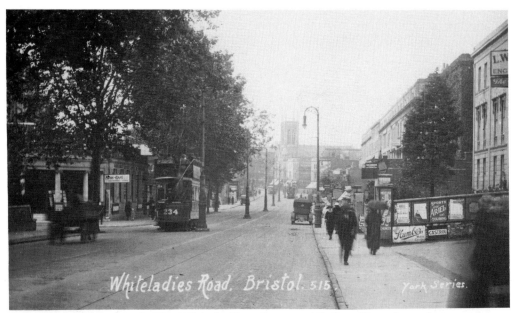

11. Whiteladies Road. The Whiteladies cinema with its pillared porch opened in 1922. A busy street scene, with Tyndale Baptist Church Tower in the distance. Postcard published in the York Series.

12. Whiteladies Road. Approaching Cotham Hill, the horse and cart on the left delivering "Rocklight" Oil, with a clear view of the overhead tram poles and wires, from the centre of the road.

13. Whiteladies Road approaching Clifton Down Station, with single storey shops now replaced by a large shopping complex. Opposite the tram are adverts for Jones Patent Flour and Twinnings Coal, and in front of the hoarding the bridge over the Temple Meads - Severn Beach railway line. Card posted 1st October 1912.

14. Whiteladies Road looking in the opposite direction to illustration 13. The single storey shops are unchanged, although this photograph was taken many years later in the early 1950s, when tram transport had been replaced by double decker buses.

15. Clifton Down Station. The staff standing on the station platform. Decorations celebrating the visit of King Edward VII and Queen Alexandra to open the King Edward Dock at Avonmouth on July 9th 1908. The station opened in 1874.

16. Clifton Down Station. The workmen in a group for the photographer, with their tressels and step ladders giving the station pillars and ironwork a fresh coat of paint.

17. Whiteladies road, on the left the turning for Clifton Down Station, adjoining the Imperial Hotel, now owned by Bristol University. Opposite a closer view of the tower of Tyndale Baptist Church. This view about 1904.

18. Blackboy Hill. The bottom of the hill, with the Wilts and Dorset Bank, now Lloyds, on the corner of Burlington Road. This 1920s view shows the tram as the main form of transport

19. Blackboy Hill. A closer look at the shops, with many sun-blinds. A summers day, although the postcard was sent in January 1906.

20. The Blackboy Inn which until 1874 stood across the road near the top of Blackboy Hill, hence the name. The Chapel building on the right remains today.

21. Blackboy Hill showing a thriving rank of shops, opposite where the Blackboy Inn once stood. This card postally used in 1912.

22. Worrall Road off of Blackboy Hill. W.H. Webber's Livery Stables, Sutherland Mews, established in 1863. The premises, which are still surviving to-day in Sutherland Place, are now used for business purposes.

23. Durdham Down Cafe, at the top left hand side of Blackboy Hill, with the manageress and staff standing outside the shop. This 1920s view with interesting window displays was next door to Gyle's Sports Shop, with the signs for sporting games on the right of this view, they are still trading today.

24. Blackboy Hill looking towards the city, the turning on the left Grove Road, with Worrall Road opposite. Published by Viner of Bath.

25. Blackboy Hill from the fountain memorial to Rev. Urijah Thomas in 1903. The many advertising hoardings include adverts for Boots the Chemist, Bovril, Cerebos Salt and Fry's Chocolate. The Kings Arms public house behind the tram and the rank of shops adjoining built in 1881. Postcard published by A.G. Short, and posted in 1918.

26. St. Johns School facing Durdham Downs, famous for the unusual tiling on the roof. Published by Burgess & Co. Bristol.

27. The Glen, a former quarry. This view shows seats filling up for a performance. The many social activities over the years include performances of military bands, and use as a dance hall.

28. The Glen in the 1950s owned then by Caroline's Cake Shop, where teas and refreshments were served. This play area was very popular. Note the growth of the trees compared with illustration 27.

29. From the top of Blackboy Hill, and St. Johns School, looking along Stoke Road. Bank Holiday crowds, with the rear view of an early open sided Bristol Tramways bus. Postcard published by Senior & Co. Motor buses replaced horse buses in 1906, and ran between the Victoria Rooms and Suspension Bridge. This view from around 1906-7.

30. Stoke Road in the opposite direction to illustration 29. The fountain on the left inscribed to George W Edwards Esquire, Mayor 1877, in the distance the houses bordering the Downs in Upper Belgrave Road. Picture from before 1910.

31. Although the caption on this postcard names the road facing the top of Durdham Downs as Belgrave Road, its correct name is Upper Belgrave Road. This view in 1918 shows a tank on display, used in the early days of the 1914-18 war on the western front.

32. Upper Belgrave Road looking in the direction of Blackboy Hill with its varied architecture of houses facing Durdham Downs. This view about 1920.

33. Upper Belgrave Road by the 'Island', near Stoke Road. Tram posts and lines visible for a distance along the road. Postcard posted on May 10th 1909.

34. Upper Belgrave Road, a carriage in the middle of the road. Postcard sent by the same person as illustration 33, on May 13th 1909. Both cards have an 'X' on them, to denote the house where the sender was staying.

35. The front entrance of Clifton Zoo, facing Durdham Downs. The Zoo opened in 1835. This view by photographer Garratt shows crowds gathering at the main entrance for a day at the Zoo. Card postally used in 1933.

36. Alfred the Gorilla, a great favourite with visitors to Bristol Zoo over many years. This scene in July 1938 by R.H. Bond.

37. Rosie the Elephant, seen here giving rides to young children with her keeper. The elephant walk was along the main promenade towards the Bear Pit and Aquarium.

The Swing at Clifton Zoo.

38. The Ivy clad lodge at the Guthre Road entrance to the Bristol Zoo, the upper part of the windows had stained glass depicting Zoo animals. This view on a postcard posted in April 1910 shows children enjoying a swing on the Maypole behind the lodge.

Upper Belgrave Rd., Clifton.

39. Upper Belgrave Road from Pembroke Road, with Downside Road the small turning on the right. The horse trough given by the Bristol and Clifton Ladies' Society of the R.S.P.C.A. in 1906.

40. The Mansion House, on the promenade was given to Bristol, for the Lord Mayor of Bristol residence by Alderman Proctor. Postcard posted from Clifton on July 13th 1904.

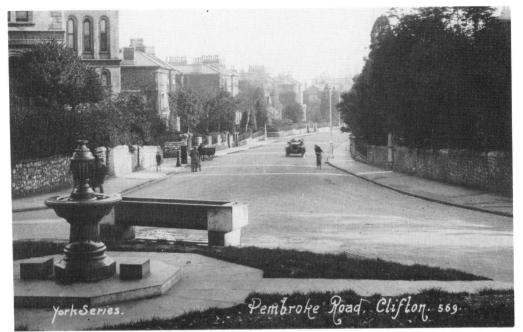

41. Pembroke Road, a sweeping view from the horse trough in illustration 39. A fountain now erected by the horse trough, the large private houses now mainly converted to offices and apartments. Picture dated about 1928.

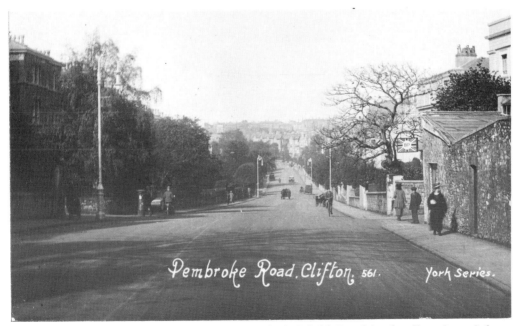

42. Pembroke Road near the junction with Oakfield Road in the direction of the Downs. A garage on the right with a patriotic "BP" petrol sign. Picture again about 1928.

43. Alma Vale Road from the corner with St. Johns Road, the tower of All Saints Church in Pembroke Road above the houses. F.E. Clapp, Fruiterer and Greengrocer on the right, and still trading in the early 1950s. This postcard posted in December 1932.

44. St. Johns Road extends parallel with Whiteladies Road, from Apsley Road to Alma Road.

45. Clifton College. The main school and headmasters house were opened in 1862, and the chapel completed in 1866, with additions in later years. The boys are playing cricket on this postally used card by Garratt in September 1925.

46. College Road which begins by the Zoo at Clifton Down, crosses Guthre Road and Clifton College and connects with Clifton Park. Many of the large houses in the road are now part of Clifton College. Postcard postally used in May 1916.

47. Proctor's Fountain at the cross-roads, at the top of Bridge Valley Road. The fountain was built to honour Alderman Procter, for his work and generosity to the citizens of Bristol.

48. Clifton Down with the tree lined promenade. The iron railings on the left and right have been removed. The rest of the view is relatively unchanged. Published by Viner of Bath.

49. St. Brenda's Nursing Home. This view is the back of the home in Christchurch Road, the nursing staff are on the verandah and Matron on the steps! The front of the building faces Clifton Park.

50. Clifton Park ivy clad cottages and elegant terraced houses beyond, facing Christ Church. A boy standing in the road with his delivery basket, and an early motor bike and side-car parked near the railings, owned by photographer Garratt. Card postally used on January 21st 1913.

51. Christ Church Clifton, from Clifton Down Road, with an early bus emerging from the direction of the Clifton Suspension Bridge. This view about 1920.

52. Cornwallis Crescent. One of the many crescents built when Clifton was being developed in the late 1790s.

53. Portland Place from Gloucester Row. Today it is all known as The Mall, crossing Portland Street and connecting with Princess Victoria Street. Picture dated about 1907.

54. The Mall from Princess Victoria Street with the offices of Midland Railway on the left. Picture dated before 1910.

55. Regent Street. A delightful group of children and delivery boys standing part-
ly in the road. This picture looks in the direction of Merchants Road and Princess
Victoria Street. Postcard published by A.G. Short & Co. in the Chatterton Series.

56. Regent Street. In the opposite direction of illustration 55, with a ladies hair-
dressing salon one of the shops on the left, with John Cordeux extended premises
opposite.

57. Regent Street in the direction of Christ Church. The turning on the right is Merchants Road.

58. Merchants Road about 1906. As the road curves right, the back view of the terraced houses in Victoria Square.

59. Waterloo Street, A narrow turning off Princess Victoria Street and connecting with Portland Street, the cart owned by James Moffat of Bedminster. The two little girls, a woman in the doorway of her shop and man holding the horse make this an interesting card. Picture taken in 1910.

60. Victoria Street (now known as Princess Victoria Street). The Mall, the turning by the boy and street lamp, Regent Street at the far end. Postcard posted in September 1908.

61. Caledonian Place. One of the many terraced roads, built when Clifton was being developed as a new area in the 1790s.

62. Royal York Crescent. Building commenced in 1791, but remained unfinished through lack of money by the builders. They were finally completed in 1818. This view by Garratt is of the Regent Street end.

63. Royal York Crescent. Associated with many famous people, Empress Eugenie (wife of Napoleon III) went to school at number 2, and at number 25 the father of Field Marshal Lord Roberts used to live. Postcard by Garratt.

64. Royal York Crescent. Some interesting fashion amongst this group of ladies around an early car. The steps leading up to the terrace of Royal York Crescent, a superb social history photograph dated September 1905.

65. Victoria Square faces a small park surrounded by iron railings, approached from Merchants Road. Card posted in June 1918.

66. Vyvyan Terrace between Lansdown Road and Clifton Park. Named after a Bristol M.P. Postcard posted in Clifton in December 1928.

67. Saville Place. A delightful curved terrace off of Regent Street, with their own pillared entrance, and private park in front.

68. Saville Place. A closer view of the terrace showing the variation in design. The small balcony extending to the more traditional covered balcony.

69. West Mall. Situated just off of the Mall, with quite a variation of architecture. The nearest balcony with hanging baskets of flowers. Postcard published by Viner of Bath, and sold locally by S.J. Thomas of Boyces Avenue.

70. West Mall. The uniform architecture and balconys, from the far end, showing the houses facing the private park which extends all the way along the road. Card postally used in May 1914.

71. Clifton Down Hotel. Opened in 1865, and also showing the houses of Gloucester Row facing Clifton Downs, the path leading in the direction of the Clifton Suspension Bridge. Picture by Garratt, about 1915.

72. Another view of Clifton Down Hotel, the lower road leading to the Suspension Bridge, and the path in the foreground to Observatory Hill. In 1766 a windmill was built for grinding snuff there, this was destroyed by fire and in 1829 the Observatory was built. (See illustration 82).

73. Sion Hill from Clifton Suspension Bridge. The houses facing the Avon Gorge, with part of the rock formation typical of the Gorge in the foreground.

74. The main entrance to the Clifton Down Hotel, with the Bristol Coat of Arms above the doorway, the building extending into Sion Place. Postcard posted in 1917.

75. The Grand Spa Hotel overlooks the Suspension Bridge and the Avon Gorge, with the entrance to the former ballroom centre left.

76. Prince's Buildings looking in the direction of Royal York Crescent from the corner of Lansdown Terrace. This card posted in April 1916.

CLIFTON

77. Clifton Rocks Railway was opened in 1893, linking Hotwells with Clifton, it was closed in 1934. Tram No. 210 awaits passengers from the railway. Posted in July 1928, but the postcard was issued quite a few years earlier.

78. Clifton Rocks Railway, the interior of the Rocks Railway. The cars were operated by water ballast, and the walls of the tunnel were brick lined. In the first weeks when it opened, many thousands of people travelled on it.

CLIFTON

79. Clifton Suspension Bridge. Designed by I.K. Brunel, the building of the bridge was started in 1831, but because of a shortage of money only the two towers were completed, one on the Somerset side, the other on the Clifton side. It remained like this until the chains from the Hungerford Suspension Bridge were purchased. Work was completed and the bridge officially opened in 1864. This view shows the bridge nearing completion in 1863.

80. The Suspension Bridge in later years showing maintenance work still going on. The workman in a cradle, is working on the stonework of the bridge. The kiosk where Ice Cream, Chocolate and Drinks could be bought by the tower of the bridge, this view looking towards the Somerset side.

CLIFTON

81. An aerial view looking over the Suspension Bridge, with the River Avon beneath. The fine terraces of Clifton, with Hotwells and the Portway below. Postcard postally used in September 1951.

82. An aerial view looking in the opposite direction, the terraces of Clifton with the Observatory on high ground right of the Suspension Bridge, across the bridge Leigh Woods. Looking down the River Avon, Sneyd Park and Sea Mills, and finally Shirehampton and Avonmouth.

83. The Avenue, also known as Birdcage Walk, the pathway is situated near the junction with Queens Road.

84. Clifton Place. A turning on the right into Queens Road towards the Victoria Rooms. The three storey Lansdown Hotel is still trading today.

85. Richmond Terrace, near the top of Queens Road connecting with Clifton Road. A terrace not much changed today, although some shops have been built under the railed pavement. Postcard published by Viner of Bath.

86. Queens Road, looking towards the Victoria Rooms, with Richmond Terrace on the right, ahead the spire of St. Pauls church in St. Pauls Road. Queens Road continues right past this junction. This brings us the full circle of our postcard tour of Clifton, which we trust you have enjoyed.

INDEX